Metamorphosis
(A Spiritual Transformation)

Scripture verses are from *The Message* written By Eugene H. Peterson, ISBN 1-57683-289-9

Copyright @ 2011 by Gary P. Monk

All rights reserved

ISBN-13: 978-1466419049
ISBN-10: 1466419040

Printed in USA by CreateSpace
www.CreateSpace.com/3703728

A worldwide spiritual awaking is happening right now.

Millions upon millions of people are hearing the Good News and accepting Jesus Christ as their Lord and Savior.

These people are your family, friends, neighbors, or maybe you and they have questions.

What is Christianity all about?
Who is Jesus?
How do I obtain salvation?
What do I do next?

Table of Contents

Table of Contents iii
Dedication iv
Introduction 1
Cosmic Battle 4
   Rules of Engagement: 6
The Journey 14
Jesus 22
Holy Spirit 27
Agape Love 32
Spiritual Warfare 37
Image of God 43
Words – Weapons of War 52
   Blessing vs. Cursing 55
   Mercy vs. Judgment 58
   Binding and Loosing 59
   Healing Vs. Sickness 60
Spiritual Principles 61
   Worship 62
   Thanksgiving 64
   Prayer 65
   Meditation 66
   Imagination 68
   Integrity 69
   Repentance 70
   Forgiveness 72
   Humility 73
   Fellowship 74
Summary 78
Acknowledgements 79
From the Author 80

Dedication

I dedicated this book to Don and Nancy Childs who I met while stationed near Saratoga Springs, New York. Don and Nancy were members at a Free Methodist Church just outside of Saratoga Springs. They opened their home to military personnel and local young adults for home group meetings.

As mentors to these young adults, Don and Nancy modeled God's unconditional love. They taught us about Jesus, the Holy Spirit and allowed us to practice what they were teaching. The greatest truth that I learned from them is that Christianity did not have to be mundane. It is a passionate and exciting adventure with Jesus.

Don and Nancy, thank you for your passion and dedication to our Lord and Savior. – Gary

Introduction

This book has two purposes. It provides a perspective on the struggle between Kingdom of God and Lucifer's Kingdom, and it offers a roadmap to guide a believer on their journey. The Bible explains that God initially created humanity in God's image. Unfortunately, Adam and Eve chose self-love rather than God's unconditional love, and they were changed from free spiritual beings into fallen beings ruled by an evil taskmaster. Their taskmaster has enslaved Adam and Eve's descendants for generations. Because God created humankind in His image, Satan has methodically and diabolically harassed humankind. The taskmaster's goal is to blind humankind to God's unconditional love. If people do not sense God's love, they will reject God and, by default, worship Satan.

Every person enters life as a non-believer and in a fallen condition. When a person chooses to believe in Jesus, he or she becomes a new creation in Christ immediately. After salvation, he or she will undergo a metamorphosis of the heart or soul from a fallen individual into the image of Christ. A metamorphic process is the transformation from one creature into another creature. One example you may be familiar with is the caterpillar to a butterfly. The unique feature of the metamorphosis process is the original caterpillar does not resemble the adult butterfly. This is different from other life cycles where the infant is a mini prototype of the adult. Kittens, puppies and babies are miniature models of their parents.

After Jesus frees the descendants of Adam and Eve from slavery, through a metamorphic process the Holy Spirit transforms the redeemed into an alien race. These new creatures become a royal priesthood for their adoptive Father. The process is not quick nor is it painless. Similar to the struggle a butterfly must undertake to escape from the chrysalis, believers must engage in a spiritual war to escape their bondage due to believing their former taskmaster's deception of love of self.

When Jesus was physically on Earth, He shared a parable about the sowing of seeds. In the parable, a farmer sowed seeds by scattering the seeds as he walked. The seeds landed in four distinct areas: the hard path, rocky ground, among thorns and thistles, and on fertile ground. As Adam and Eve's descendants, your free will determines the type of soil our heart contains. (Luke 8:4-15)

People that have hardened their hearts to unconditional love are the hard pathway. They reject Jesus' message of unconditional love. Shallow individuals with little strength of character are the rocky ground. They initially receive the gospel message, but the experiences of the transformation process cause them to fall away. People consumed by normal life are the soil with thorns and thistles. They accept the concept of the gospel and show up for church to sit in the pews. Only Jesus knows if they are spiritually dead or alive. Individuals who embrace the transformation process are the fertile ground. They yearn to know Jesus intimately. If you want more of Jesus, read on!

Cosmic Battle

Did you ever wonder how an all-powerful loving God could create an angel that chose to become the manifestation of evil?

Is it possible that when God creates from His essence, unless He replicates Himself, He cannot infuse the creation with the fullness of His attributes? Any creation without all of God's attributes has the ability to act differently than God. Rather than manifesting God's selfless, unconditional, agape love, Lucifer chose love of self.

Lucifer introduced self-love into God's creation. Picture in your mind a third of creation controlled by evil. There is no freedom, only slavery. All of creation is groaning to be free. Everything that was good is perverted. Love became selfishness, peace became control, hope became fear, and passion became lust. Fallen angels or demons torment, manipulate, and terrorize creation.

God put into action His plan to redeem creation. The two thirds of the angels uncorrupted by self-love drove Lucifer (Satan) and the other fallen angels out of heaven. After being defeated, Satan bargains with God to keep his freedom.

Satan says, "You know that your creation will never love you."

God replies, "Oh, I think you are mistaken."

Satan snipes back, "Sure, if you buy their love with all kinds of gifts, they might think that they love you, but in reality it will only be because you bought their affection."

God chuckles and says, "Lucifer you still don't understand that agape love is the most powerful force in creation."

Satan sneers, "That may be true, but you require holiness, and your creation will make mistakes. Therefore you will never have intimacy with them."

God responds, "Lucifer, before I pass judgment on you for rebelling, I will prove to you that love conquers all."

Satan responds with glee, "If I win, I get to keep dominion over the first heaven."

God smiles and agrees.

Satan senses a trap and insists "Hold on, we need some clear rules. You cannot just cause creation to love you."

Again, God smiles and agrees. "My creation will have a free will. Shall we begin?"

Rules of Engagement:

1) Lucifer can only use deception to convince a person to reject God's love. (Jn 8:44)
2) Any lie believed will result in negative consequences. Fallen angels (demons) will enforce these consequences (curses). Demons pass curses on to the fourth generation. (Ex 34:7)
3) God can only use truth to convince a person to believe in the unconditional love of God (Jn 8:32)
4) Any truth believed will result in positive consequences. Ministering spirits (angels) will apply these positive consequences (blessing). Angels pass blessings on for a thousand generations. (Deut. 7:9)

5) A spoken word has the power of life or death. The degree of power will depend on the amount of emotional passion empowering the spoken word (faith). (Prov. 18:21)
6) Emotional (heart) beliefs are more powerful than intellectual beliefs. Emotional beliefs determine whether a person responds with unconditional love or self-love. (Luke 6:45)

In the war between good and evil, God chose the soul of humankind as the cosmic battleground. God placed Adam and Eve in the Garden of Eden on the planet Earth, knowing they would be deceived by self-love. When Adam and Eve chose self-love over selfless love, they became fallen beings because the Holy Spirit departed, and God banned them from the Garden of Eden. After the fall, Satan and his demons unleashed their deception and torment on humanity.

Two thousand years ago, God reestablished a beachhead on planet Earth. Through fallen humanity, God chose to demonstrate the power of unconditional love by sending His only Son Jesus to be born into a world controlled by self-love. Born of a fallen virgin, Jesus entered the world fully human. From the moment of Jesus' birth, everything that He did and said imparted agape love into the fallen world.

Satan thought this was his chance to secure victory. He took his best shot at Jesus. Satan tempted and tormented Jesus using the same methods he uses on the rest of humanity. Through every temptation, Jesus modeled agape love. When Satan could not get Jesus to choose self-love, he decided to kill Jesus.

After being tempted as fully human, Jesus freely gave Himself as a sacrifice to redeem all of fallen creation. "This is how much God loved the world: He gave His Son, His one and only Son. And this is why: so that no one need be destroyed; by believing in Him, anyone can have a whole and lasting life. God did not go to all the trouble of sending His Son merely to point an accusing finger, telling the world how bad it was. He came to help, to put the world right again. Anyone who trusts in Him is acquitted; anyone who refuses to trust Him has long since been under the death sentence without knowing it." (JN 3:16&17)

When Adam and Eve chose self-love in the Garden of Eden, they forfeited their spiritual heritage and became fallen beings. Through His life, death, and resurrection, Jesus gives everyone an opportunity to regain their spiritual heritage as children of God. In the third chapter of the Gospel of John, Jesus explains that we must be born again. Jesus defines this as being born of the spirit where the Holy Spirit resides within you. When you are born again as a spiritual being, you instantly become a child of God.

In Romans, the Apostle Paul wrote, "This resurrection life you received from God is not a timid, grave-tending life. It is adventurously expectant, greeting God with a childlike 'what's next, Papa?' God's Spirit touches our spirits and confirms who we really are. We know who He is, and we know who we are: Father and children. And we know we are going to get what is coming to us—an unbelievable inheritance! We go through exactly what Christ goes through. If we go through the hard times with him, then we're certainly going to go through the good times with Him!"
(Rom 8:15-17)

The focal point of the cosmic battle is whether an individual is born again in the spirit. Every salvation is a victory. In Colossians, the Apostle Paul wrote, "God rescued us from dead-end alleys and dark dungeons. He's set us up in the kingdom of the Son he loves so

much, the Son who got us out of the pit we were in, got rid of the sins we were doomed to keep repeating."
(Col 1:13-15)

For all humanity, God is engaged in a continual battle to demonstrate to people that accepting Jesus as Lord and Savior is the only way. For thousands of years, Satan has spread lies, fear, hate, lust and greed. Fortunately, God relentlessly pursues us. "Don't overlook the obvious here, friends. With God, one day is as good as a thousand years, a thousand years as a day. God is not late with his promise as some measure lateness. He is restraining himself on account of you, holding back the end because he does not want anyone lost. He's giving everyone space and time to change."
(2 Peter 3:8&9)

Every person must continuously make choices as life is lived. On your life journey, God uses events, literature, art, nature, and struggles to get your attention. He calls you to respond to His unconditional love. You may see God's interactions as coincidences, acts of nature, or simply consequences. In His mercy, God directly intervenes with miracles, prophecies, and through other people modeling unconditional love in your relationships. God desires to stir a yearning in your heart to want agape love. It is believed that all of their descendants genetically remember Adam and Eve's experience with the Holy Spirit. People describe it as a hole in your heart that only God's agape love can fill.

In the cosmic battle for your soul, every person chooses between unconditional love and self-love. The choice can be either a passive non-decision or an active decision. For some, the decision does not come until their deathbed and for others it is made early in life. Since humankind resides in self-love territory, all non-decisions belong to Satan. Satan's trump card is he wins by default. You must make a conscious decision to accept Jesus as Lord and Savior. Satan also wins when you do not select Jesus. You may not realize you are rejecting unconditional love and accepting spiritual death. You believe Satan's lies that you can find true love without God. Lastly, you have a free will, and like Satan, you may openly chose evil.

For an individual who chooses to accept Jesus' gift of salvation, the Holy Spirit returns to reside within them. At this point, you are spiritually born again. The birth process does not produce a mature spiritual being. It simply begins the transformation of your fallen mind into the image of Christ. However, God is sovereign, and He can accelerate spiritual growth as we allow Him.

Have you made a decision? Are you willing to take a chance that unconditional love is better than self-love?

In third chapter of Romans, Paul presents the Gospel.

"Since we've compiled this long and sorry record as sinners and proved that we are utterly incapable of living the glorious lives God wills for us, God did it for us. Out of sheer generosity, He put us in right standing with Himself. A pure gift. He got us out of the mess we are in and restored us to where He always wanted us to be. And He did it by means of Jesus Christ.

God sacrificed Jesus on the altar of the world to clear that world of sin. Having faith in Him sets us in the clear. God decided on this course of action in full view of the public—to set the world in the clear with Himself through the sacrifice of Jesus, finally taking care of the sins He had so patiently endured. This is not only clear, but it is now—this is current history! God sets things right. He also makes it possible for us to live in his rightness." (Rom 3:23-26)

Once Jesus wins the cosmic battle for your heart, the Holy Spirit begins a metamorphic process to convert your self-love into unconditional agape love. The Apostle Paul states, "Instead, fix your attention on God. You will be changed from the inside out. Readily recognize what he wants from you, and quickly respond to it. Unlike the culture around you, always dragging you down to its level of immaturity, God brings the best out of you, develops well-formed maturity in you." (Rom 12:2) Like Jesus' disciples, as you learn to walk in agape love you grow as a child of God effectively demonstrating and spreading God's agape love.

Your change from a fallen creature to a child of God forces Satan to change his deceptive tactics. Rather than getting you to ignore the Gospel of Christ, Satan focuses on disempowering your walk with Jesus. However, by pursuing and submitting to the transformation process, you will allow the Holy Spirit's power and love to flow though and out of you, changing you from a fallen creature into the image of Christ.

The Journey

(From where you are to where you will be)

Before God created Lucifer, your Heavenly Father knew you. He knew the role you would play in the cosmic battle to redeem creation. When God created you, He gave you gifts and purposes to fulfill. Satan has taken every opportunity to confuse, manipulate and deceive you in an effort to subvert your purposes. With every lie you believed, every curse placed on you, every judgment or vow you made, and every sin you committed Satan sought to change God's original design. God foreknew how Satan would try to destroy you. God in His mercy redeems what Satan tried to destroy and uses it to empower you. The transformation into the image of Jesus Christ occurs as the Holy Spirit works within you to redeem what the enemy has stolen and destroyed. The Holy Spirit takes all the pain and brokenness you have experienced by living in the fallen creation and causes them to work for your good. (Rom 8:28) The transformation process is not a single event, but a life long journey.

On your journey, you are going to experience many kinds of trials. Satan uses these experiences to plant doubt in your mind. When life happens and you see disasters, illnesses, poverty, war, slavery, illegal sex traders, and pedophiles, Satan may place a question in your mind. Why would a good loving God cause these things to happen?

When Satan rebelled, a third of creation fell with him. The fallen portion of creation ceased to function with God's perfect order and chaos ensued. Since Lucifer rebelled, the fallen area has been decaying. God's creation is longing for redemption and elimination of chaos. The Apostle Paul wrote in Romans, "The created world itself can hardly wait for what's coming next. Everything in creation is being more or less held back. God reins it in until both creation and all the creatures are ready and can be released at the same moment into the glorious times ahead. Meanwhile, the joyful anticipation deepens." (Rom 8:19-21) Your Heavenly Father wants to redeem not only humankind, but also all of fallen creation.

Since the Earth is decaying, the laws of nature that govern the geophysical and ecological balance on Earth are failing. The Earth is dying as it waits for God's redemption. Since humankind lives on Earth, people will experience the death struggles of earthquakes, hurricanes, floods, droughts, pestilence, and other disasters. These combined with failing interpersonal relationships will create all kinds of trials and tribulations. A poem, titled *Footprints in the Sand* summarizes God's response to these trials.

One night a man had a dream. He dreamed
he was walking along the beach with the LORD.
Across the sky flashed scenes from his life.
For each scene, he noticed two sets of
footprints in the sand: one belonging
to him, and the other to the LORD.
When the last scene of his life flashed before him,
he looked back at the footprints in the sand.
He noticed that many times along the path of
his life there was only one set of footprints.
He also noticed that it happened at the very
lowest and saddest times in his life.
This really bothered him and he
questioned the LORD about it:
"LORD, you said that once I decided to follow
you, you'd walk with me all the way.
But I have noticed that during the most
troublesome times in my life,
there is only one set of footprints.
I don't understand why when
I needed you most you would leave me."
The LORD replied:
"My son, my precious child,
I love you and I would never leave you.
During your times of trial and suffering,
when you see only one set of footprints,
it was then that I carried you."
Anonymous

While Jesus is carrying you, He sings love songs and woos you with unconditional love. Your spirit knows God did not create you for chaos. During a crisis or trial, your heart is more open to and yearning for your Heavenly Father's unconditional love. James, Jesus' brother, encourages you to use this spiritual trait to benefit from trials and tribulations.

"Consider it a sheer gift, friends, when tests and challenges come at you from all sides. You know that under pressure, your faith-life is forced into the open and shows its true colors. So do not try to get out of anything prematurely. Let it do its work so you become mature and well-developed, not deficient in any way." (Jas 1:2-4)

The wonderful thing about the transformation process is that it is the Holy Spirit's responsibility to transform you. The Apostle Paul wrote in Philippians, "There has never been the slightest doubt in my mind that the God who started this great work in you would keep at it and bring it to a flourishing finish on the very day Christ Jesus appears." (Phil 1:6)

When you choose to be "born again," the Holy Spirit comes to reside within you. Instantly, the Holy Spirit changes you from a fallen creature into a child of God. With proper nourishment, you will grow and change your natural characteristics into spiritual attributes. The Holy Spirit will guide you into all truth. Your Heavenly Father loves you so much that the Holy Spirit will never leave you or forsake you. Regardless of your struggles, the Holy Spirit will always comfort, guide and encourage you. Unconditional love only builds up. It does not tear down or destroy.

Life continually presents you with choices. When you choose to respond with God's unconditional love, you become more like the image of Jesus. When you respond in self-love, you have the opportunity to learn what does not glorify Jesus. Even when you fail, the Holy Spirit builds up and encourages. You cannot earn God's love, and you cannot lose His love. Jesus does not want you to stop sinning under your own power. He wants you to respond to His agape love and your sins will no longer hold you in bondage. As Jesus releases you from bondage, the sins fall away and you will reflect the image of Christ.

In Philippians, the Apostle Paul provides a roadmap to keep you on the road to the image of Christ. It states:

"Celebrate God all day, every day. I mean, revel in him! Make it as clear as you can to all you meet that you are on their side, working with them and not against them. Help them see that the Master is about to arrive. He could show up any minute!

Do not fret or worry. Instead of worrying, pray. Let petitions and praises shape your worries into prayers, letting God know your concerns. Before you know it, a sense of God's wholeness, everything coming together for good, will come and settle you down. It is wonderful what happens when Christ displaces worry at the center of your life.

Summing it all up, friends, I'd say you'll do best by filling your minds and meditating on things true, noble, reputable, authentic, compelling, gracious—the best, not the worst; the beautiful, not the ugly; things to praise, not things to curse. Put into practice what you learned from me, what you heard and saw and realized. Do that, and God, who makes everything work together, will work you into his most excellent harmonies."
(Phil 4:4-9)

The Book of Exodus is the story of God freeing the Israelites from slavery and leading them on a journey to freedom in the Promised Land. During their journey to the Promised Land, God transformed the Israelites from slaves into a powerful army capable of driving out the kingdoms that occupied the Promised Land. Your testimony is your personal Book of Exodus. It will describe your journey with the Holy Spirit as you metamorphose from a slave in Satan's fallen kingdom into a Royal Priest of your Creator God.

Jesus

(Fully God and fully man)

Who is Jesus? He is the Son of God, and He is fully man and fully God. Jesus has all the attributes of God the Father: His holiness, purity, righteousness, compassion, long suffering, joy, unconditional love, mercy, and much more. Jesus is endless and infinite. As fully man, Jesus came to Earth to redeem creation. To accomplish this task, Jesus modeled agape love, offered Himself as a redeeming sacrifice, arose from the dead, and ascended to heaven. Each action broke the power of a satanic strong hold.

Jesus' ministry on Earth transformed His disciples from common fishermen to powerful ambassadors that turned the world upside down. Jesus mentored and modeled agape love to disciples. Jesus gradually released responsibilities to disciples as he trained them and sent them out as ambassadors to surrounding communities.

Jesus' healing ministry demonstrated that God desires everyone to walk in health and freedom. In

Matthew chapter 10, Jesus gave His disciples authority to heal every kind of disease and every kind of sickness. In addition, Jesus overruled the traditions of man and healed on the Sabbath.

On the way to the cross, Jesus provided for your healing, covered your sins, and bore your suffering. Isaiah wrote, "He was looked down on and passed over, a man who suffered, who knew pain firsthand. One look at Him and people turned away. We looked down on Him, thought He was scum. But the fact is it was our pains He carried— our disfigurements, all the things wrong with us. We thought He brought it on Himself, that God was punishing Him for His own failures. But it was our sins that did that to Him, that ripped and tore and crushed Him—our sins! He took the punishment, and that made us whole. Through His bruises, we get healed. We are all like sheep that have wandered off and gotten lost. We have all done our own thing, gone our own way. And God has piled all our sins, everything we've done wrong, on Him, on Him (Jesus)." (Isa 53:3-6)

After His death, Jesus descended into hell and set the captives free. Jesus led all believers who died before His death out of hell and escorted them to heaven. This broke the power and bondage of sin and death. Jesus' ascension to heaven and promise of His return gives believers a hope of eternal life.

Jesus said that when people saw Him, they saw the Father. As a believer, your goal is when people see you, they see Jesus' unconditional love.

WAIT! Do not give up. It is not as difficult as Satan wants you to believe. Jesus' brother Jude wrote, "And now to him who can keep you on your feet, standing tall in his bright presence, fresh and celebrating—to our one God, our only Savior, through Jesus Christ, our Master, be glory, majesty, strength, and rule before all time, and now, and to the end of all time. Yes."
(Jude 24&25) Similarly, the Apostle John wrote, "But they're no match for what is embedded deeply within you—Christ's anointing, no less! You do not need any of their so-called teaching. Christ's anointing teaches you the truth on everything you need to know about yourself and him, uncontaminated by a single lie. Live deeply in what you were taught." (I John 2:26&27)

You are powerless to become the image of Christ. The harder you try to become the image of Christ the more religious and self-righteous you become. This does not imply that all you have to do is go sit on a mountaintop and wait for God to change you. The Holy Spirit will literally take you by the hand and guide you through the transformation process. However, for this to happen, you need to open your heart to Him and listen to His guidance.

The Apostle Matthew wrote in his gospel, "Steep your life in God-reality, God-initiative, and God-provisions. Do not worry about missing out. You'll find all your everyday human concerns will be met." (Matt 6:33) A powerful truth is learning to ask WHAT God wants you to learn rather than WHY is this happening.

The power of Jesus' unconditional love transformed His disciples from individuals walking in self-love to spiritual soldiers filled with agape love. The process Jesus used to change His disciples from ordinary men into the most powerful army ever assembled will change you from a new believer into a royal priesthood. The second chapter of First Peter states: "But you are the ones chosen by God, chosen for the high calling of priestly work, chosen to be a holy people, God's instruments to do his work and speak out for him, to tell others of the night-and-day difference he made for you—from nothing to something, from rejected to accepted." (1 Pet 2:9-10)

The practical implications of Jesus loving you include eternal rewards and rewards here on Earth. It seems that most of the rewards associated with believing in Jesus come when you arrive in heaven. Fortunately, while you are on Earth, Jesus provides you with weapons to defend yourself against the enemy of your soul. As you learn to use these weapons effectively, you will experience tangible benefits.

The most common earthly benefits are the fruit of the spirit listed in Galatians, "But what happens when we live God's way? He brings gifts into our lives, much the same way that fruit appears in an orchard—things like affection for others, exuberance about life, serenity. We develop willingness to stick with things, a sense of compassion in the heart, and a conviction that a basic holiness permeates things and people. We find ourselves involved in loyal commitments, not needing to force our way in life, able to marshal and direct our energies wisely." (Gal 5:22&23)

Holy Spirit

(Helper – Comforter)

In Philippians, the Apostle Paul explains that when Jesus was born on Earth, "Jesus had equal status with God but didn't think so much of Himself that He had to cling to the advantages of that status no matter what. Not at all. When the time came, He set aside the privileges of deity and took on the status of a slave, became human!"(Phil 2:6&7) For 30 years, Jesus lived fully human without the Holy Spirit residing within Him. During this time, Jesus experienced the temptations of Satan without sinning.

At the beginning of His ministry, Jesus went to John the Baptist to be water baptized. During Jesus' water baptism, the Holy Spirit descended on Jesus and resided within Him. Jesus, being fully human, allowed the Holy Spirit to manifest Its power though Jesus to perform miracles. During Jesus' ministry, He healed the sick, cast out demons, and raised the dead by the power of the Holy Spirit residing in Him.

In John's Gospel, Jesus said, "You will do even greater works than He did." Jesus knew that the power to perform miracles was the Holy Spirit residing within Him and functioning through unconditional love. After Jesus' resurrection, He sent the Holy Spirit to indwell every believer.

When a person accepts Jesus as Lord and Savior, the Holy Spirit indwells that person. All the power and authority available to Jesus during His ministry on Earth is available to every believer. Satan does not want any believer to walk in the power and unconditional love of the Holy Spirit, so he uses every trick in his arsenal to deceive and disempower believers.

One of the greatest benefits to you is the Holy Spirit helping you in your weaknesses. In Romans, the Apostle Paul wrote, "Meanwhile, the moment we get tired in the waiting, God's Spirit is right alongside helping us along. If we do not know how or what to pray it does not matter because the Holy Spirit does our praying in and for us, making prayer out of our wordless sighs, our aching groans. He knows us far better than we know ourselves, knows our pregnant condition, and keeps us present before God. That's why we can be so sure that every detail in our lives of love for God is worked into something good." (Rom 8:26-28) Just imagine the power of the Holy Spirit praying for you through you.

This explains why Satan does everything he can to discredit praying in the Spirit and speaking in tongues. If the Holy Spirit, who is God, intercedes for you to God the Father in accordance with the Father's will, your Heavenly Father will act on your behalf. Fortunately, accessing speaking in tongues for personal prayer, or praying in the Spirit, is available to every believer. Allowing the Holy Spirit to pray through you requires an act of your free will.

Since the Holy Spirit already resides within you, the ability to pray in the Spirit requires two actions on your part. First, acknowledge to yourself that the Heavenly Father wants you to have good gifts and praying in tongues is a good gift. Second, with the intent to glorify God, begin speaking syllables that have no meaning to you and trust the Holy Spirit to put meaning to the sounds. Imagine the Holy Spirit is a reservoir of water inside of you and praying in the Spirit allows the water to flow. As a lake's outlet river keeps the lake water fresh, praying in the Spirit keeps your soul fresh by identifying and removing your weaknesses.

In I Corinthians, the Apostle Paul wrote, "If I pray in tongues, my spirit prays but my mind lies fallow, and all that intelligence is wasted. So what is the solution? The answer is simple enough. Do both. I should be spiritually free and expressive as I pray, but I should also be thoughtful and mindful as I pray. I should sing with my spirit, and sing with my mind." (I Cor. 14:14&15)

Rest assured the Holy Spirit wants your mind to be fruitful. After praying in tongues for a few minutes, stop and ask the Holy Spirit what He wants you to know about that intercession. As you calm your mind, you can listen for spontaneous thoughts or a still small voice. It is beneficial to write these down. As you learn to hear from God, obtain feedback from other Christians on what you hear to determine how God speaks to you.

The most powerful weapon a believer has is being able to recognize your Heavenly Father's voice. The Apostle John quoted Jesus as saying, "I'm not making this up, but speaking only what the Father taught me." (Jn 8:28) Jesus never sinned because He always recognized and listened to His Heavenly Father's voice, not because Jesus used His deity powers as the Son of God.

Agape Love

In Antioch, around 55 A.D., people began calling believers Christians. The word Christian means like Christ. The Antioch believers learned agape love by seeing the love modeled by believers who knew Jesus personally.

Have you ever participated in a "telephone game?" I remember in grade school, we would play during recess. We would sit in a circle and someone would start by saying a phrase to the child next to him or her. The phrase would pass from child to child until it completed the circle. Then, the last child would say the phrase aloud, and the originating child would restate the original phase. The group would laugh at how much the phrase changed.

Like the telephone game phrase, Christianity for many slowly changed. While unintentional, the modifications affected how believers' modeled unconditional love. Subtle but critical aspects of the Christian life were lost to many. Satan deceived the body of Christ with lies that changed the church's image of God. The righteousness, power, and authority of the church and the ability to continue to turn the world upside down for Jesus were lost in many areas.

When people lost the true image of God, they turned to religion. They created organizations and traditions to reach the world. Intellectual knowledge became more important than intimacy with the Holy Trinity. Division and strife fractured the Body of Christ. Ultimately, the term Christian became synonymous with critical and judgmental, and the Body of Christ began to model the very self-love they loathed. Without the agape love of the Father, Son and Holy Spirit, much of the Body of Christ has nothing to offer a lost and suffering world.

Concerning the cosmic battle, the Apostle Paul wrote in Second Corinthians, "The world is unprincipled. It's dog-eat-dog out there! The world does not fight fair. But we do not live or fight our battles that way—never have and never will. The tools of our trade are not for marketing or manipulation, but they are for demolishing that entire massively corrupt culture. We use our powerful God-tools for smashing warped philosophies, tearing down barriers erected against the truth of God, fitting every loose thought and emotion and impulse into the structure of life shaped by Christ. Our tools are ready at hand for clearing the ground of every obstruction and building lives of obedience into maturity." (II Cor. 10:3-6)

Many in the Body of Christ fight as the world fights. They tear down, judge and criticize anything that does not fit into their perceptions of Christianity. Each person acts as if they know what God thinks and wants. They defend their ideas without regard to the foundation of Christianity, unconditional love.

The Prophet Isaiah challenges this know it all approach to God. God says, "I don't think the way you think. The way you work isn't the way I work.' God decrees, 'For as the sky soars high above earth, so the way I work surpasses the way you work, and the way I think is beyond the way you think." (Isa 55:8&9)

The Apostle Paul supports Isaiah, "God can do anything, you know—far more than you could ever imagine or guess or request in your wildest dreams! He does it not by pushing us around but by working within us, His Spirit deeply and gently within us." (Eph 3:20)

In an epistle, the Apostle John wrote about the importance of walking in agape love. "My beloved friends let us continue to love each other since love comes from God. Everyone who loves is born of God and experiences a relationship with God. The person who refuses to love does not know the first thing about God, because God is love—so you cannot know Him if you do not love. This is how God showed His love for us: God sent His only Son into the world so we might live through Him. This is the kind of love we are talking about—not that we once upon a time loved God, but that He loved us and sent His Son as a sacrifice to clear away our sins and the damage they have done to our relationship with God.

My dear, dear friends, if God loved us like this, we certainly ought to love each other. No one has seen God, ever. But if we love one another, God dwells deeply within us, and His love becomes complete in us—perfect love!

This is how we know we are living steadily and deeply in Him, and He in us: He has given us life from His life, from His very own Spirit. Also, we have seen for ourselves and continue to state openly that the Father sent His Son as Savior of the world. Everyone who confesses that Jesus is God's Son participates continuously in an intimate relationship with God. We know it so well, we have embraced it heart and soul, this love that comes from God.

God is love. When we take up permanent residence in a life of love, we live in God and God lives in us. This way, love has the run of the house and becomes at home and matures in us, so that we are free of worry on Judgment Day—our standing in the world is identical with Christ's. There is no room in love for fear. Well-formed love banishes fear. Since fear is crippling, a fearful life—fear of death, fear of judgment—is one not yet fully formed in love.

We, though, are going to love—love and be loved. First, we were loved; now we love. He loved us first.

If anyone boasts, 'I love God,' and goes right on hating his brother or sister, thinking nothing of it, he is a liar. If he will not love the person he can see, how can he love the God he cannot see? The command we have from Christ is blunt: Loving God includes loving people. You've got to love both." (1 Jn 4:7-21)

Spiritual Warfare

As a person, you have three distinct characteristics: your mind, which includes your emotions, your physical body, and your spirit. Satan wants to steal, kill, and destroy these. First, Satan wants to steal your spiritual heritage as a child of God. Satan steals your heritage by attacking the other two areas. If possible, Satan will kill your physical body before you accept Jesus. While he is trying to kill you, he destroys your mind with lies and deception to keep you from accepting Jesus.

In the Gospel of Luke, "An expert in Biblical law asked Jesus, 'What must I do to inherit eternal life?'

Jesus responded with a question, 'What is written in the Law?'

The individual answered, 'Love the Lord your God with all your heart and with all your soul and with all your strength and with your entire mind; and love your neighbor as yourself.'

Jesus replied, 'You have answered correctly. Do this and you will live!" (Luke 10:25-28)

You are at the proverbial point in a difficult situation.

Can you unconditionally love God and your neighbor? In reality, no you cannot. Therefore, you cannot fulfill the law and inherit eternal life.

Fortunately, the Apostle Paul rallies to your defense by proclaiming, Christ abolished the law and replaced it with grace. Paul repeatedly states that you cannot fulfill the law. Therefore, in your own strength, you cannot love God and your neighbor as yourself. In the fifth chapter of Paul's letter to the Galatians, Paul emphatically states rather than trying to be good enough for God, focus on allowing the Holy Spirit to lead you. Christianity is not about your behavior; it is about surrendering to God's unconditional love and responding in your spiritual nature. The Apostle Paul calls it a circumcision of the heart.

Personal spiritual warfare is your internal struggle between responding with your fallen nature and responding with your redeemed spiritual nature. When you respond in your fallen nature, you commit a sin. While the Bible has many words to describe sin, it is acting on an ungodly belief instead of God's truth. Your sin is the symptoms or manifestation of what you believe.

Ungodly beliefs come from believing the lies that Satan and people manipulated by Satan tell you. Young children are emotionally innocent and susceptible to believing lies. During painful life events, Satan uses lies to encourage children to create defense mechanisms with ungodly beliefs. While these individuals believe their defense mechanisms will protect them, in reality the defense mechanisms bind the experience to their emotional pain. Any similar experience will cause the individual to feel the suppressed emotional pain.

Emotional pain is one of Satan's most powerful tools that he uses to control and manipulate people. The old saying, "Sticks and stones may break my bones, but words will not hurt me" is a lie. For years, Satan has been tormenting and inflicting you with pain. Satan uses wounded people to wound other people. You may be familiar with the term "pushing your buttons." Satan uses people to push your buttons and tap into your suppressed emotional pain. When you are in a painful emotional state, Satan feeds you additional lies.

Ungodly beliefs or lies are like poison ivy or weeds. Once believed, it spreads rapidly throughout your mind influencing memories and beliefs. The cycle of deception and manipulation Satan uses to reinforce these ungodly beliefs is similar to addiction. Many addictions start with an individual innocently trying something new. The substance stopped the pain and the individual tries it again. Eventually, it takes more and more to stop the pain. Then, the addiction controls you.

Once you believe the lie, Satan has a foothold and he feeds you additional lies. When you accept an ungodly belief, it decreases your ability to differentiate between what is truth and what is a lie, which makes you susceptible to believing ungodly beliefs. As the number of ungodly beliefs you believe increases, your true self is suppressed. Ultimately, the lies you believe control you.

Satan uses many different schemes to feed you lies unforgiveness, bitterness, pride, abuse, exploitations, judgments, unmet expectations, greed, lust, anger, or fear. These ungodly beliefs act as spiritual shackles. Satan can push that emotional pain button anytime he wants you to respond in your fallen nature. As long as you believe these lies, you are essentially Satan's puppet.

The metamorphic process is the transformation of your beliefs from ungodly beliefs to Godly beliefs. The Apostle Paul says, "So here's what I want you to do, God helping you: Take your everyday, ordinary life—your sleeping, eating, going-to-work, and walking-around life—and place it before God as an offering. Embracing what God does for you is the best thing you can do for him. Do not become so well adjusted to your culture that you fit into it without even thinking. Instead, fix your attention on God. You will be changed from the inside out. Readily recognize what he wants from you, and quickly respond to it. Unlike the culture around you, always dragging you down to its level of immaturity, God brings the best out of you, develops well-formed maturity in you." (Rom 12:1&2)

The Apostle Paul warns you in Romans, chapter seven, that during your life journey, your sin will trip you up. Remember, Christ's sacrifice covers any response of your fallen nature. However, the Apostle Paul goes on to say do not use your freedom in Christ to indulge in self-gratification and pain avoidance.

Why not? If you are lonely, stressed, depressed, or hurting, Satan encourages these types of behaviors because they will numb your pain. Then, Satan uses your guilt and shame to numb your awareness of the Holy Spirit, which limits your ability to follow the Holy Spirit's leading. These shortcuts to stop emotional or spiritual pain keep your fallen nature alive and slow your metamorphic process.

As your guide and helper, the Holy Spirit uses the metamorphic process to remove the lies and bondages that Satan uses to embed the pain. Without the pain, it is easier for you to avoid responding with your fallen nature. Your new spiritual nature can respond in unconditional love.

The process Satan uses to enslave your fallen nature leaves two very visible telltale signs that reveal his shackles of deception disproportionate emotional pain, an overreaction to an insignificant event, and sinful behaviors. It is possible to follow these signs to the ungodly belief where Jesus can speak truth into your spirit and break the shackle, setting you free.

Image of God

A person's belief about God's attributes shapes his/her image of God. You formed your image of God by gathering information as you lived your life. The resulting perception of God is a summation of everything you believe. While Christianity promotes a personal relationship with God, your personal image and awareness of God directly affects the type of relationship you have with God.

To connect with God, each person must examine his/her personal image of God and compare it to the God presented in the Bible. The following ten multiple-choice questions provide you with an opportunity to clarify your image of God. It is important to select your answers based on what you feel is true, not on what you think is correct. There are no wrong answers. The choices provided are only to stimulate your thinking. The blank choice (e) is for you to consider other possible answers.

Take some time to read the questions and meditate on each answer. As you contemplate the answers, focus on your feelings. If an answer feels true, write it down on a separate sheet of paper. Each question can have multiple answers that feel true even if the answers seem to contradict each other. For choice (e) read the question and ponder what feels true. You are not looking for an intellectual definition, but an emotional perception of what feels true. Be honest with yourself.

1. I feel that God is:
   a) Always there
   b) Busy
   c) Expectant
   d) Involved
   e)
2. I see God as:
   a) All powerful
   b) A Judge
   c) Affectionate
   d) Attentive
   e)
3. I envision God as being:
   a) Holy
   b) Everywhere
   c) Inflexible
   d) Indifferent
   e)
4. I believe God is:
   a) Compassionate
   b) Watching
   c) Aloof
   d) Unchanging
   e)

5. I sense that God is:
   a) Hard to please
   b) All knowing
   c) Faithful
   d) Forgiving
   e)
6. I perceive God as being:
   a) Full of grace
   b) Demanding
   c) Understanding
   d) A perfectionist
   e)
7. When I hear God loves me, I feel:
   a) Accepted
   b) Confused
   c) Invisible
   d) Like a disappointment
   e)
8. I imagine that God is:
   a) Incredible
   b) Gentle
   c) Always with me
   d) Too good to be true
   e)

9. I picture God as being:
   a) Loving
   b) Tough
   c) Firm
   d) Relentless
   e)
10. I visualize that God is:
    a) Joyful
    b) Holding me
    c) Dancing with me
    d) Disappointed with me
    e)

Your compiled list of words and phrases provides you with an impression of how you view God. Do you wonder how it compares with how the Bible presents God?

For centuries, scholars have gleaned God's attributes from the Bible. However, they do not all agree on the number of attributes. Some scholars identify less than ten, and others say God has up to an infinite number of attributes. Rather than looking at a list of words, take a few minutes and read three abbreviated stories in the

Bible that describe peoples' reactions to an encounter with God.

Isaiah described a vision of God, "I saw the Master sitting on a throne—high, exalted!—and the train of His robes filled the Temple. Two angel-seraphs called back and forth, Holy, Holy, Holy is God-of-the-Angel-Armies. God's bright glory fills the whole earth.

Isaiah exclaimed, 'Doom! It is Doomsday! I'm as good as dead!" (Isa. 6:1-5)

The Apostle John, Jesus' beloved disciple who laid his head on Jesus' chest, described an encounter with the ascended Lord Jesus. "I saw a gold menorah with seven branches, And in the center, the Son of Man, in a robe and gold breastplate, hair a blizzard of white, eyes pouring fire-blaze, both feet furnace-fired bronze, His voice a cataract, right hand holding the Seven Stars, His mouth a sharp-biting sword, His face a perigee sun.

I saw this and fainted dead at His feet. His right hand pulled me upright, His voice reassured me: Do not fear: I am First, I am Last, I am Alive. I died, but I came to life, and my life is now forever." (Rev 1:12-18)

Mark's Gospel describes Jesus' return to His hometown of Nazareth and the people's response to Jesus. "Jesus said, 'A prophet has little honor in his hometown, among his relatives, on the streets he played in as a child.' Jesus wasn't able to do much of anything there—He laid hands on a few sick people and healed them, that's all." (Mk 6:4-5) The Nazarenes' saw Jesus as one of them.

These descriptions of personal encounters with God create two very different images. The Apostle John and Isaiah experienced a being of incredible majesty and awe-inspiring glory, which instilled complete reverence. The Nazarenes experienced a common man and distained Him.

Since the Garden of Eden, Satan has striven to water down man's image of God. For generations the Jewish people would not write the name of God, let alone say it. During that time, Israel and the surrounding nations revered the God of Israel. In today's culture, humanity regularly uses God's name as profanity and God is not revered. The Body of Christ must honor God's image to affect the culture around the Body of Christ.

The restoration of the reverence of God in the church and your nation's culture starts with you the individual. God wants you to have a true image of Him. Take your compiled a list of words or phrases and ask yourself the following question. Does your image of God agree with what the Bible states about God? If you are not sure, ask your mentor or a Pastor you trust.

Once you have identified the ungodly beliefs that do not agree with the Bible, take them to God and ask Him to reveal His truth. Your mentor, or Pastor, can assist you with surrendering these ungodly beliefs to God.

Jesus stated, "Make them holy—consecrated—with the truth; God's word is consecrating truth." (Jn 17:17) As you pursue God's truth in the Bible with an open heart and mind, God will reveal His truth and break the bondages of your ungodly beliefs. Once your image of God portrays Him as Holy, Awesome, Majestic, and All-powerful, your words will be a powerful weapon to release God's truth and unconditional love into a fallen and dying world.

How you view God affects your ability to incorporate spiritual principles into your life and allow those principles to transform you into the image of Christ. As you delve into the spiritual principles, humbly ask the Father God to reveal His character and attributes to you. The refining process will continue as long as you are alive on Earth.

Words – Weapons of War

The premise of this chapter is Proverbs 18:21 "Words kill, words give life; they are either poison or fruit—you choose." The power of life and death in your words may sound unrealistic, so this chapter is going to examine scriptures that demonstrate that your words will bring either life or death.

To understand the power of words, look at God's creation of Earth. God used the spoken word to create everything. Imagine God being in the utter darkness of fallen creation and saying "let there be light." Suddenly without defining how, there was light. The amazing thing is God created the sun later. Now, that is a God thing. How is there light without a source? Oh, God is the source. That defines creative power. God's creative power is so incredible; the universe is still creating new stars billions of years later.

When God created humankind, God said, "Let us make human beings in our image, make them reflecting our nature so they can be responsible for the fish in the

sea, the birds in the air, the cattle, and, yes, Earth itself, and every animal that moves on the face of Earth."
(Gen 1:26)

When God created humankind in His image, He infused humankind with spiritual attributes. These attributes included the authority and power of words. The amount of power a word contains depends on the amount of faith you have that it will fulfill its purpose. When God speaks, His words create what God said because He has infinite faith in Himself.

Faith is a mystical word that sometimes defies definition. At a fundamental level, faith is a combination of intellectual beliefs and heart-felt convictions. Your mind balances intellectual knowledge, believing, and emotional conviction to create faith. Beliefs fueled by heart-felt convictions are powerful. Jesus states, "I know you inside and out, and find little to my liking. You are not cold; you are not hot—far better to be either cold or hot! You are stale. You are stagnant. You make me want to vomit." (Rev 3:15) Without heart-felt conviction, your intellectual beliefs are stale and powerless.

From a cosmic battle for the souls of humanity perspective, the authority of the spoken word is like a hydrogen bomb. People continuously speak words to create manifestations of either unconditional love or self-love. Every person has a choice of how to use that power. Everyone, Christians, new agers, and witches have access to the power and authority. When a person speaks, his/her faith determines whether the spoken word will happen. Since God created people in His image, humanity's faith can be in himself or herself, God, or Satan.

There should be signs around the community stating "Speaker Beware." With your words, you complain, make vows, express judgments, place curses, break promises, tell lies, and criticize people. Words, like seeds, take root and grow. When you sow seeds, you will reap from ten to a hundred fold. Satan manipulates and deceives people into doing his bidding. Sadly, Satan uses people as weapons to spread lies, kill, and destroy other people.

Your spiritual war is against Satan and his demons. It is not against people created in the image of God. Consider, God unconditionally loves every person, and desires for every person to come to a saving knowledge of Jesus. As God's Royal Priest, you can release God's blessing on people. When you bless sinners, political leaders, or your enemies, you are God's agent in redeeming these people.

For believers, the Holy Spirit amplifies the power of their spoken word. As you open your heart and allow the Holy Spirit to speak through you, you release God's creative power. Your worship, prayer, encouragement, and spiritual warfare bring glory to your Heavenly Father and releases agape love into the fallen world. Your words empowered by the Holy Spirit have the power to bind the enemy and release God's holy attributes into any situation. At the Holy Spirit's direction, you can speak words of compassion to stop a hurt, or share your testimony to an unbelieving individual.

Blessing vs. Cursing

James, the brother of Jesus, wrote, "A word out of your mouth may seem of no account, but it can accomplish nearly anything—or destroy it!

It only takes a spark, remember, to set off a forest fire. A careless or wrongly placed word out of your mouth can do that. By our speech, we can ruin the world, turn harmony to chaos, throw mud on a reputation, send the whole world up in smoke, and go up in smoke with it, smoke right from the pit of hell.

This is scary: You can tame a tiger, but you cannot tame a tongue—it has never been done. The tongue runs wild, a wanton killer. With our tongues, we bless God our Father; with the same tongues, we curse the very men and women he made in his image; Curses and blessings out of the same mouth! My friends, this can't go on." (James 3:4-10)

A blessing or a curse is calling something that is not as if it were. With your creative power, your words can bring into existence whatever you say. The question you must ask yourself is do I want to bring good or evil with my words. As with everything, the choice is yours.

James states, "God is impervious to evil, and puts evil in no one's way." (James 1:14) If God does not put evil in your way, then He will never use you to tempt or destroy someone else. Unfortunately, Satan does want to use you to tempt and destroy people. When you catch yourself using your words to curse someone, repent and ask Jesus to reveal the root cause and speak truth into your heart.

When you are blessing someone, declare God's purpose and intention into his or her life with passion, hope, and expectation. Blessing someone is not an idle common event. You are standing at the throne of your heavenly Father and requesting the He alter the course of history for the person you are blessing. Put your heart into your words and mean what you say.

Another powerful use of the spoken word is to proclaim truth over yourself and your family. When you, an adopted child of God, speak into the supernatural realm, ministering spirits take action to fulfill your words. The best source of truth is the Bible. For example, "Jabez prayed to the God of Israel, Bless me, O bless me! Give me land, large tracts of land. And provide your personal protection—do not let evil hurt me. God gave Jabez what he asked." (1 Chron. 4:9&10)

Similarly, Jesus used the Lord's Prayer to teach His disciples how to proclaim blessing over their lives. God is a loving, good God who has the power and desire to fulfill your proclamations. Select several of your favorite scriptural promises and daily proclaim them over yourself and your family.

Fortunately, wherever you are in your journey with God, your Heavenly Father wants you to know He loves you as you are and is not disappointed with you. God simply encourages you to seek first His selfless love. As you experience God's agape love, your responses will convey unconditional love. As you pursue God's unconditional love, the Holy Spirit will bring you to places of repentance, forgiveness, and breaking vows and curses. The Holy Spirit wants you free, and the He will redeem every one of your self-love motivated words.

Mercy vs. Judgment

When God created you in His image, He gave you the ability to judge. With the ability to judge comes great responsibility. As a judge, you must evaluate all of the facts related to the situation you are judging. Unfortunately, as a non-omniscient creation, you cannot know all facts associated with a situation. Therefore, you cannot judge fairly. Jesus warns you about judging, "Judge not unless you want to be judged." (Matt 7:1)

Fortunately, James provides you with an alternative to judging. He states, "Kind mercy wins over harsh judgment every time. When you catch yourself judging someone, you should acknowledge that you judged and ask Jesus to forgive you. After you have repented, ask Jesus to release His mercy and blessing into the life of the other person.

Binding and Loosing

While your spiritual authority is a powerful weapon, it is a double-edged sword. As an agent of Christ, you have the authority to bind on Earth. However, the emphasis of the Bible is granting freedom. God's light and truth always drive out darkness. When you focus on releasing God's attributes and promises into a situation, Satan will flee. A critical key to spiritual victory is your heart motive and passion.

Healing Vs. Sickness

A spiritual image of sickness is a serpent coiled around an organ or person crushing the life out. While the serpent will have legal ground to inflict the illness, Jesus paid for the healing at Calvary. "But He was pierced through for our transgressions, He was crushed for our iniquities; the chastening for our well-being *fell* upon Him, and by His scourging we are healed." (Isa 53:5) As with everything when praying for healings, we know in part. It is important to rely on the Holy Spirit to guide our prayers. By releasing God's presence into the situation and asking the Holy Spirit how to pray, you are tearing down strong holds and bringing freedom into the person.

Spiritual Principles

Spiritual principles are personal disciplines that when practiced with an attitude of humility and surrender open an individual's heart to the leading of the Holy Spirit. The intent of this section is to provide an introduction of these principles. Hundreds, if not thousands, of books are available to provide a lifetime of study on these topics.

Christianity is not about mastering any discipline. Rather the focus is getting to know your Heavenly Father at a deeper intimate level. Satan understands that intimacy with God is the source of all truth, so Satan will do anything to prevent your intimacy with God.

Satan has learned that if he claims to be the source of a discipline or gift the church shuns and avoids those gifts. A couple of examples are meditation and imagination. Satan has tried hard to convince the church that those are his tools. The truth is that God is the creator of all things, and Satan is a counterfeiter and a liar.

As you learn to develop any spiritual discipline, you must always be aware of the spiritual battle you fight. Satan has two primary weapons to confront spiritual principles: distractions and compulsion. With distractions, Satan strives to use your flesh to diminish the value of developing a spiritual discipline by getting you to focus on other wants. With compulsions, Satan attempts to push you to extremism. Allowing either weapon to interfere with your pursuit of God will hinder your relationship with Him.

In Psalm 46:10, God says, "Cease striving and know that I am God." A quiet time can include many different disciplines, such as worship, prayer, meditation, being still, reading God's word, and waiting on God. As with everything associated with seeking God, your intent to glorify God and to be open with your spirit is important.

Worship

It seems that people have a propensity to worship. People worship athletes and movie stars, beauty, nature, success, cars, objects, social and political positions, and the list goes on. If you take a step back and wonder why people need to worship, you may acknowledge that people subconsciously realize they are not the pinnacle of existence.

The Holy Trinity created everything including Lucifer. As the Creator God, He deserves and desires worship. Worship is the reverent love and devotion freely given to God. Even Jesus worshiped His Heavenly Father in the Lord's Prayer, where Jesus started with "Our Father who is in heaven, holy is your name."

True worship is more than singing songs. It is adoration of the Father, Son and Holy Spirit. Adoration requires an opening of your spirit in humility and surrender to acknowledge and appreciate all the Holy Trinity has done for you. It is visualizing God's awesome attributes and immeasurable goodness and thanking Him for showering His love on you. Realizing even as you contemplate your insignificance, the Heavenly Father lifts you up and places you in His lap to love you unconditionally.

Thanksgiving

One of the most powerful forms of worship is thanksgiving. Psalm 100 is a psalm for giving grateful praise, "Enter with the password, Thank you! Make yourselves at home, talking praise. Thank Him. Worship Him. For God is sheer beauty, all generous love, loyal always and ever." (Ps 100:4&5) The Bible offers many examples of humanity offering praise and thanksgiving to God. A Biblical word study will reveal how God's people have worshipped and praised Him.

Life with all of its trials and tribulations can easily overshadow the blessing that God provides. Satan tries hard to get people into the pity party. In the Old Testament, the Jewish people are infamous for complaining about their situation to God. Part of the metamorphic process is learning to be thankful even in difficult times.

Another word that reflects thanksgiving is contentment. The Apostle Paul wrote in Philippians, "Actually, I don't have a sense of needing anything personally. I have learned by now to be quite content whatever my circumstances. I am just as happy with little as with much, with much as with little. I have found the recipe for being happy whether full or hungry, hands full or hands empty. Whatever I have, wherever I am, I can make it through anything in the One who makes me who I am." (Phil 4:11-13)

Prayer

Before you open your mouth to pray, always check your spirit for your motive. Compassionate, heartfelt prayers of faith release God's power and unconditional love into any situation. When you pray, remember to ask for God's unconditional agape love to flood the focus of your prayers. Miracles of power and healings get peoples' attention, but it is God's unconditional love is eternal. As the Apostle Paul wrote in I Corinthians, chapter 13, "Without love I am nothing."

In the Lord's Prayer, Jesus said "Thy (the Father's) will be done on Earth as it is in heaven." When in prayer, take a moment to consider this point. If we are honest with ourselves, there are many situations where we only have opinions about what is best. Ask yourself, "Do I know the Father's will?" If not, pray in tongues and let the Holy Spirit pray though you. After praying in tongues, ask the Holy Spirit to reveal what He prayed though you. Then, pray it with your words. It is better to allow the Holy Spirit to pray through you rather than praying against God's will.

Meditation

As with every spiritual discipline, meditation starts with the intent to glorify God. Meditation is the art of mulling over in your mind a truth or principle. A major difference between being still and meditation is with meditation your can explore spontaneous interruptions.

Meditation helps you look at yourself and learn what you really believe. Satan has been feeding you lies your whole life. When you believe these lies, they become your truth. There is a difference between an experiential lie and an intellectual lie. For example, an experiential lie occurs when Satan tells you that you are unlovable during a traumatic event. These are ungodly beliefs. An intellectual lie occurs when a person tells you, "I did not take your drink," when in fact they did take it.

People are very complex, and you can intellectually believe one thing and emotionally believe contradicting ungodly beliefs at the same time. In behaviors, ungodly beliefs normally overrule the intellect. Since God gave humankind a free will, accepting Jesus as your Savior does not automatically remove the lies and ungodly beliefs you believe.

Removing any experiential lie requires a decision on your part to allow Jesus to speak truth in place of the lie. Jesus will not override your free will. The transformation process is getting your heart and mind to believe the same things about God's unconditional love.

You may be wondering how to determine what ungodly beliefs you believe. The Bible is a wonderful source of truth. During your meditation time, ask yourself how you feel about Biblical truths. Phrase your questions with an open-ended statement like, "God is good, except when... Jesus would love me if... By asking yourself these types of questions in an emotionally safe place, your subconsciousness can answer with what you believe experientially.

If your beliefs do not agree with scripture, ask Jesus to reveal His truth to you experientially. In addition, you should work with a trusted companion who has experience with resolving ungodly beliefs. After you learn to hear Jesus speaking His truth, you will be able to reveal ungodly beliefs during your meditation time.

Imagination

Imagination is looking into the future. It is from where dreams or fears come. Fear is allowing your imagination to focus on the negative, and dreams are focusing on God's power and deliverance. God uses your imagination to provide creativity, visions and dreams to guide you on your journey. In addition, God can use your imagination to break the power of lies that Satan has convinced you are true.

It may be difficult to envision yourself in God's lap. However, laying your head on His chest is possible. Envision yourself laying your head on Jesus' chest and listening to the beating of His heart. As you quietly surrender to Jesus, ask Him to speak truth to your hurts. When you are willing to embrace the pain of a memory,

Jesus will take you to the memory where Satan lied to you and reveal truth.

Integrity

Paul wrote whatever is true, whatever is noble, whatever is right, whatever is pure, whatever is lovely, and whatever is admirable, think about such things. For a person to display integrity, they must be true to themselves. Since Satan has deceived, manipulated, and controlled you most of your life, it can be difficult to recognize what is truth. Thankfully, the Holy Spirit will guide you into all truth. However, it does require you to pursue the truth.

The pursuit of truth requires an honest personal inventory of who you are spiritually, emotionally, and behaviorally. Satan will try to convince you to hide your secret sins. Sins kept in secret grow. Fortunately, the good news is that God already knows you and He loves you exactly as you are today. When you can confess your sin to yourself, God and a trusted friend, it takes the sin out of the darkness into the marvelous light. This is the first step in breaking the bondage of that sin.

It is not about performance; it is about surrender. Remember, God does not need you to change for Him. He wants you to change for yourself. As you trust and love God and become transparent, your sins will fall away.

The power of an honest inventory is the freedom that comes from being real before God. In addition, you get to see the incredible changes happening in your life as you pursue loving God. Do not be fooled by Satan's favorite lie that once you find truth you can help fix other people. In truth, if you cannot fix yourself, how can you fix other people? God healed you by grace so that you can love other people, not fix them.

Repentance

You sin because of the ungodly beliefs that you believe are true. You believe ungodly beliefs because you accepted Satan's lie that it would protect you or give you pleasure. Like an addiction, Satan has convinced you that you need your sin. Satan's lies undermine your God given gifts and supplant your God given purpose.

Take a moment and count the number of times "you" and "your" appeared in the previous paragraph. This is important because you chose to believe the lies. People do not sin because of their parents or the devil made them do it. You sin because you chose to believe a lie.

To repent, acknowledge that you responded inappropriately out of self-love and ask the Holy Spirit to show you what you received as payment for choosing to sin. Release the payment and ask the Holy Spirit to replace what Satan stole from you.

In Psalm 32, King David describes the power of repentance. First, he tried to hide his sin, and then he repented. "Count yourself lucky, how happy you must be— you get a fresh start, your slate's wiped clean. Count yourself lucky— God holds nothing against you, and you are holding nothing back from him. When I kept it all inside, my bones turned to powder, my words became daylong groans. The pressure never let up; all the juices of my life dried up. Then I let it all out; I said I will make a clean breast of my failures to God. Suddenly the pressure was gone— my guilt dissolved, my sin disappeared." (Ps 32:1-5)

Forgiveness

In Africa, hunters capture baboons by drilling a hole in a rock and placing fruit in the hole. The hole is large enough for the baboon to slide an open hand into the hole, but small enough to trap a closed fist. Once the baboon has the fruit in its hand, it will not let it go even though it means the baboon cannot escape. Satan uses the same strategy to capture you. When you experience a perceived or real injustice, the offender owes you an apology, compensation, or something. Unless you let go of what the offender owes you, Satan will snare you and lead you into bitterness and bondage.

While creating your personal inventory, ask yourself who owes me acceptance, respect, kindness, love, gentleness, money, time, listening, advice, or comfort, and who took from me without permission? With who are you angry? Who has offended you?

Are you willing to open your hand and let them go free? It does not imply what they did was right. It does not mean you have to let them do it again. It simply means that you are getting out of the way and letting your loving Heavenly Father redeem the situation. God wants you free to love one another.

Humility

Your willingness to lay down your wants and to respond in unconditional love is true humility. In the gospel of Luke, "Jesus told them what they could expect for themselves: Anyone who intends to come with me has to let me lead. You are not in the driver's seat—I am. Do not run from suffering; embrace it. Follow me and I will show you how. Self-help is no help at all. Self-sacrifice is the way, my way, to finding yourself, your true self. What good would it do to get everything you want and lose you, the real you? If any of you is embarrassed with me and the way I am leading you, know that the Son of Man will be far more embarrassed with you when he arrives in his entire splendor in company with the Father and the holy angels. This is not, you realize, pie in the sky by and by. Some who have taken their stand right here are going to see it happen, see with their own eyes the kingdom of God."
(Luke 9:23-27)

Jesus requires that you let Him lead. This can mean saying no to your wants and yes to uncomfortable choices. It also requires you to ask yourself a question. Why am I choosing this response? Internal motives are more important than external behaviors. Some organizations promote a "Fake it until you Make it" mentality. This only works if your motive for faking is to surrender to Jesus. If you are trying to meet the expectations of the organization, faking it will not change your heart.

Fellowship

Two men were on a camping trip enjoying nature and spending quality time together. The younger man said, "All I need is the quiet open spaces and I would have a wonderful relationship with God." The other man stood up without saying a word and walked to the fire. Using a branch, he rolled a burning log out of the fire. After a few minutes, the recently removed log began to burn less brightly. Eventually, the log's flames died out. The young man looked up and said, "I understand."

The author of Hebrews states, "Let's see how inventive we can be in encouraging love and helping out, not avoiding worshiping together as some do, but spurring each other on, especially as we see the big Day approaching." (Heb 10:24&25) Fellowship can be divided into three categories: corporate worship, small group meetings, and "one, to, one" interactions.

The most recognizable corporate worship is the weekly church services at your local church. These services provide attendees with the ability to interconnect socially and spiritually. Other forms of corporate worship are conferences and musical concerts.

A New Testament meeting style of small group meetings is reemerging in the American churches. Individuals meet in homes with a smaller sub-group from their local church. The smaller group size provides Christians an opportunity to follow the Apostle Paul's advice, "So here's what I want you to do. When you gather for worship, each one of you is prepared with something that will be useful for all: Sing a hymn, teach a lesson, tell a story, lead a prayer, and provide an insight. If prayers are offered in tongues, two or three is the limit, and then only if someone is present who can interpret what you are saying. Otherwise, keep it between God and yourself. Allow no more than two or three speakers at a meeting with the rest of you listening and taking it to heart. Take your turn, no one person taking over. Then, each speaker gets a chance to say something special from God, and you all learn from each other. If you choose to speak, you are also responsible for how and when you speak. When we worship the right way, God does not stir us up into confusion; he brings us into harmony. This goes for all the churches—no exceptions." (I Cor. 14:26-33)

    The "one, to, one" relationship is a critically important aspect of fellowship. Solomon, the son of King David, wrote, "As iron sharpens iron, so one person sharpens another." (Prov. 27:17) The name of "one to one" relationships varies from organization to organization. The function of a mentor, a sponsor, or a spiritual guide is to walk alongside someone and support him or her as he/she seek intimacy with the Holy Trinity. Your mentor is not responsible for your journey. Rather he/she listens and encourages you as you seek to understand God's truth for yourself.

Your Christian journey is about obtaining freedom from the lies and ungodly beliefs you believe. Having a mentor you trust will provide you with a safe haven to be brutally honest with yourself. Through a spiritual position of surrendered transparency, an open and receptive heart has the ability to reveal your doubts, fears, and failures, which will bring them out of the darkness and into the light. Once you identify and acknowledge a lie, Jesus can speak truth into your spirit and break the bondage of the lie.

Summary

The Father, Son and Holy Spirit love you and communicate with you continuously. As you open your heart to what God is saying, He will draw you closer and closer to Himself. Seek to open your heart and hear God wooing you into intimacy with Him. As you respond in love, your behaviors will change to radiate the image of Jesus.

As you continue on your metamorphic process, always remain open to God's truth from many different sources. God can manifest His unconditional love through nature, friends, events, circumstances, and disasters. As the Apostle Paul encouraged you seek to remain content in whatever the decaying world throws at you. God's agape love is a shield and defense against the enemy's lies and deception.

Jesus encourages you to, "Seek the kingdom of God and God's true image and everything He has to offer will be added to you."

Acknowledgements

Alison, Kristen, and Dana thank you for proofreading the manuscript.

Ruth, Daryl and Jim your spiritual insight and clarifications on scriptural truths were invaluable.

Northway Care Night leaders and attendees your passion for God's truth and willing to pursue it modeled a journey after the heart of God. Thank you.

From the Author

I felt lead to write *Metamorphosis, A spiritual Transformation*, to be one of the sparks for the great spiritual awakening that is coming to this nation. My prayer is that God will use this book to bring truth into your life and set you free spiritually.

If this book helps you, please give a copy of the book to an individual who is seeking to have deeper intimacy with our Heavenly Father. You can order as many copies as you need online.

www.CreateSpace.com/3703728

Thank you,

Gary P. Monk
Last Hope Ministries
Last.Hope.Min@gmail.com

Made in the USA
Charleston, SC
11 February 2012